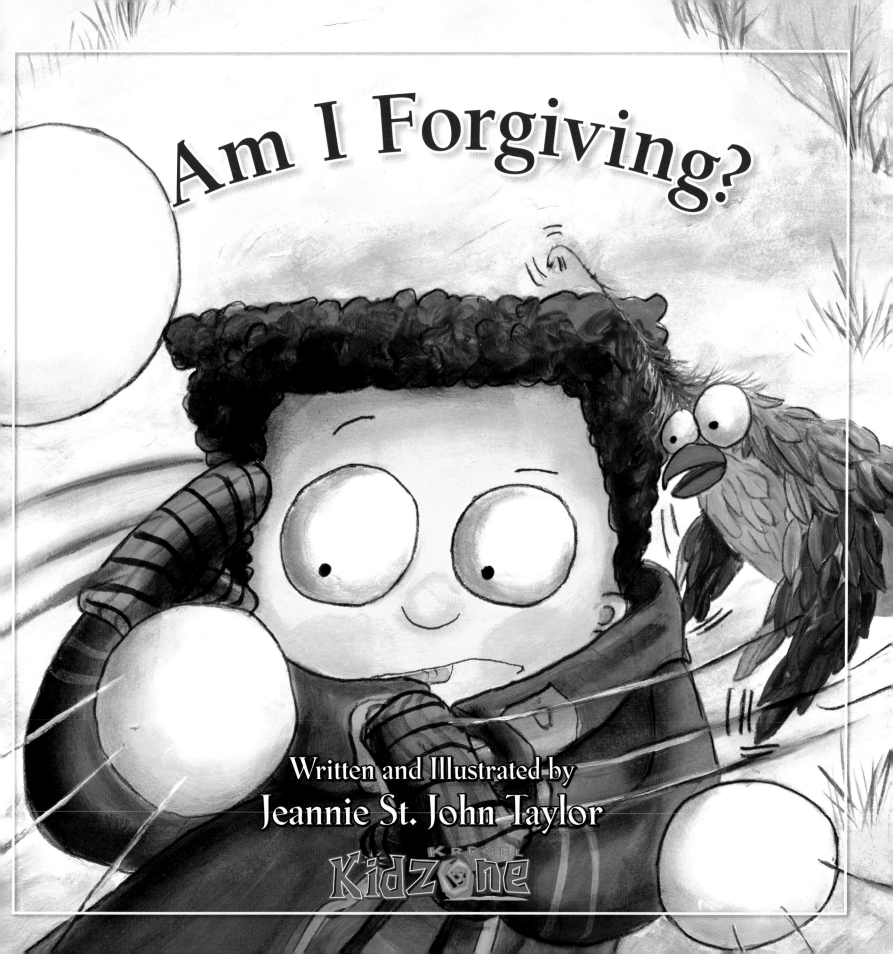

Am I Forgiving?

Written and Illustrated by

Jeannie St. John Taylor

KREGEL Kidzone

**Jeannie would love to hear from you.
She answers all e-mails personally.
She can be reached at Jeannie@kregel.com.**

Am I Forgiving?

© 2007 by Jeannie St. John Taylor

Published by Kregel Kidzone, an imprint of Kregel Publications, Grand Rapids, Michigan 49501.

Scripture taken from the *Holy Bible*, New Living Translation, copyright © 1996, 2004. Used by permission of Tyndale House Publishers, Inc., Wheaton, Illinois 60189. All rights reserved.

ISBN 10: 0-8254-3659-1
ISBN 13: 978-0-8254-3659-8

Printed in China

To the Barclift clan:
Stevie, Wesley, Jann, Elaina,
Angela, and Hannah Banana.

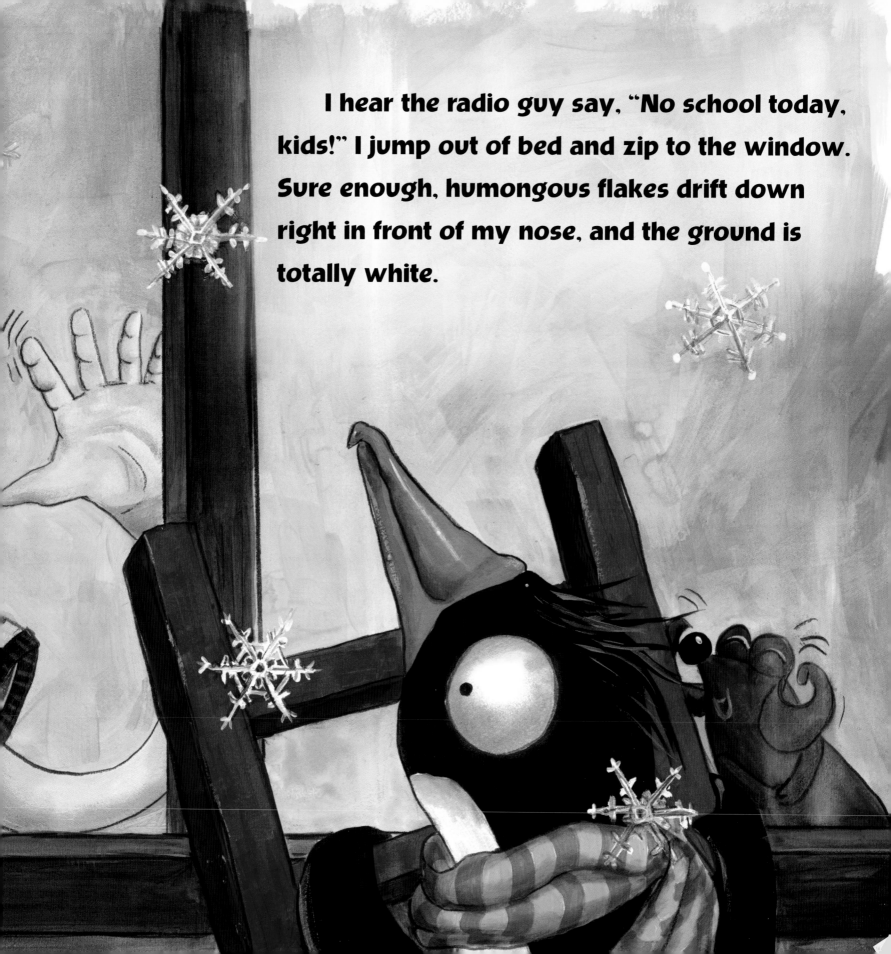

I hear the radio guy say, "No school today, kids!" I jump out of bed and zip to the window. Sure enough, humongous flakes drift down right in front of my nose, and the ground is totally white.

I grab the phone and call my best friend. I yell,
"Chuck! Meet me at the mailbox in five minutes!"
He says, "Uh . . . Todd slept over last night.
I'm gonna play with him."

I feel a little lonely, but I decide to forget about it and not hold a grudge against Chuck. That's forgiving, isn't it? Even though he didn't actually do anything to me?

I eat breakfast and haul my sled out of the garage. I
see Chuck and Todd outside. A smile springs up deep in my
tummy and skates to my face. I grin and wave, but they take
off running in the other direction.

I hurry after them, but they're speeding so fast, I can't catch up. I see Todd plop his sled onto the crest of Broke Leg Hill and zoom down, swerving around trees. He plows past the Barclift twins.

I yell, "Hey! Wait up!" Chuck glances back at me, but he doesn't stop. I feel bad for a second. Then I decide I won't be mad at him. That's forgiving, isn't it?

I throw my sled onto the snow and
whoosh down after them. I'm finally closing in
on my friends. Boy, will they be happy to see me!
The twins get so excited, Stevie hops around cheering
and Wesley rolls over and makes a snow angel.

Suddenly, snowballs come out of nowhere
and smack me in the face.

The snow gets in my eyes and I can't *see* anything. When I reach up to brush the snow away, my mitten slips off. I try to grab it, but I can't. That makes me lose control of the sled. I careen down the hill faster and faster, screaming, "Heeeeeeeeeelp!"

Wham! I slam into something that knocks me off my sled. Pain shoots up my arm and my insides feel all shivery. I hear the Barclift twins laughing.

As soon as I catch my breath, I wipe snow from my eyes and look at the thing I whammed into. A tree. But I *see* something that's lots worse—Chuck and Todd laughing at me.

My stomach hurts so much, I barely notice the pain in my arm. I ask God to help me forgive them for laughing when my arm is maybe broken.

Todd points at me and says, "Boo hoo hoo! Baby Erik is crying!"
I notice I really do have tears on my face, so I quickly turn my
head. Chuck ignores me, and when Todd says, "Let's go, Chuck," my
best friend snatches up his sled and they dash off together. I hear
them hollering and laughing as they disappear over the next hill. I
don't have time to stop crying and forgive anyone.

I leave my sled and trudge up the hill. When I get
partway, the Barclift twins come over and tell me they're
sorry they laughed. Stevie's lower lip quivers. He says,
"I didn't mean to hurt your feelings."

Wesley says, "Me neither."

I say, "That's okay, guys. I'm not mad." And I'm really not.
That proves I already forgave them, doesn't it? It's not hard to
forgive them, because they weren't mean on purpose.

The walk home takes forever. So does the drive to the doctor's office. But once the doctor puts my arm in a cast, it doesn't hurt much.

On the way home we pass the hugest snowman I've ever seen. Chuck and Todd crouch beside it, piling up snowballs so they can have a snowball fight without me.

I look straight ahead, pressing my lips together and clenching the fist on my arm that isn't broken. I'll make them sorry. I'll never let Chuck be my best friend again.

At home, Mom brings me hot chocolate and pops a cartoon in the DVD player. While I watch, I think of a hundred ways to get even with Chuck and Todd.

The problem is, I remember the Bible says that if we don't forgive others, God won't forgive *us*. I pray, "They were mean and I don't want to forgive them, Jesus, but I will if you help me. I can't do it if you don't."

About that time, the doorbell rings. It's Chuck, and he's got my sled. Anger boils up inside me and I want to say something mean. Instead, I pray, "Lord, help me forgive him."

Chuck comes inside, but he won't look at me. He says, "Sorry, Erik."

I don't say, "That's all right" or "You didn't mean to." I just say, "I forgive you." That's okay, isn't it? God doesn't expect me to pretend Chuck didn't do anything wrong.

Chuck asks if we can be best friends again. I want to say something like, "Are you kidding? Cousin Sloan is my best friend." But I don't, because I know if I try to get even, that means I'm not forgiving.

So I say, "Okay. Wanna sign my cast?" I'm offering forgiveness, aren't I? Even though I still feel a little hurt?

We have an awesome time the rest of the afternoon. I know it
might be a long time before I can totally forget all the bad things
Chuck did, but I plan to keep forgiving him every time one of them
pops into my brain . . . even if I have to forgive him hundreds of
times every day.

Hey! Do you think that's what *Jesus* means by forgiving seventy
times seven?

For Parents

God instantly forgives when we confess our sins and repent; yet we often refuse to forgive the ones who hurt us. Refusing to forgive results in bitterness that damages our character and limits our usefulness to God. Additionally, Jesus warns, "If you forgive those who sin against you, your heavenly Father will forgive you. *But if you refuse to forgive others, your Father will not forgive your sins*" (Matt. 6:14–15, emphasis added).

Read it together

As you read the story with your child, notice that though Erik forgives Todd, he does not reconcile with him. Forgiveness does not require you to trust or become good friends with the person who hurt you.

Talking it over

Thinking about getting even with someone indicates an unwillingness to forgive that person. Discuss with your child times when you found it difficult to forgive others and times when your child found it difficult to extend forgiveness.

Taking action

Does your child feel emotional pain when remembering a time someone mistreated him or her? If your child is old enough to write, ask him or her to write down the details of the incident on a sheet of paper. Then discuss the matter together. If the other person did a bad thing, say so, and do *not* say it was okay. It wasn't. But help your child forgive by deciding not to get even. Ask your child to do as God commands and pray for the person instead (see Matt. 5:43–45).

Just for fun

Instruct your child to tear the sheet of paper on which he or she recorded a painful memory into little bits and toss it into the trash as a tangible sign that your child chooses to forgive. Remind your child to forgive every time the hurtful incident pops into his or her mind. Tell your child it may be a long time before he or she stops remembering what happened, but if your child keeps praying for the person, the pain that accompanies the memory will eventually leave.

To learn more about forgiveness, e-mail the author at Jeannie@kregel.com.